W9-AWZ-567

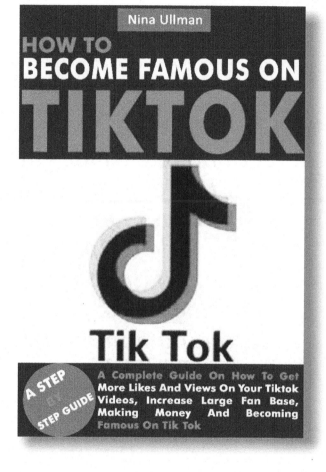

Nina Ullman

HOW TO
BECOME FAMOUS ON
TIKTOK

Tik Tok

A STEP BY STEP GUIDE

A Complete Guide On How To Get More Likes And Views On Your Tiktok Videos, Increase Large Fan Base, Making Money And Becoming Famous On Tik Tok

HOW TO BECOME FAMOUS ON TIK TOK

A Complete Guide On How To Get More Likes And Views On Your Tiktok Videos, Increase Large Fan Base, Making Money And Becoming Famous On Tik Tok

Nina Ullman

DEDICATION

This is book is specially dedicated to both older TikTok users and of course the new members.

I also dedicate this book to you. Yes, you reading this book. May your aim of getting this be achieved.

TABLE OF CONTENT

HOW TO BECOME TIK TOK FAMOUS

INTRODUCTION

Okay, folks!

I am sure you are all geared up to know how to get famous as a TikToker; there is no other person in a better position to answer every one of your questions than myself here.

Before we begin, you might want to know why I consider myself eligible to write on how you can become TikTok famous. The answer is simple. I have been an avid user of the TikTok platform since mid-2018, and I happen to be one of the crowned and verified users on the platform. Need I say more?

Now that I have cleared the air on that, let's get right into what TikTok app is.

WHAT IS TIKTOK/MUSICAL.LY?

Tik Tok is a video creation and sharing application launched in 2017. The launch of this new social media platform was met with incredibly fast reception, especially among internet users who are teenagers. With more than one billion downloads of the

Android application, the Tik Tok ecosystem is vast, diverse and is, for many users, a path to fame and fortune.

It is a short video creation application in which you can entertain others by creating music videos, dialogues and humorous videos with lip sync. With this app, you can create short videos that are 3 to 15 seconds long and upload them to entertain others.

TikTok was previously known as Musical.ly and has recently been renamed to TikTok. In fact, a Chinese company "Douyin" bought Musical.ly and merged it with its app popularly known as TikTok. On the newly launched platform, you will find many songs and dialog boxes, allowing you to make good videos from mobile devices. You will also find an editing option. The videos on the TikTok platform are quite short and fun.

This application has become very popular around the world in a very short period. Like YouTube, you can get a large number of followers by uploading good comical videos on Tik Tok and making money with them. For instance, TikTok has many popular stars such as Faisal Shaikh, Jannat Zubair and Mrunal Panchal, who have more than 10 million followers and make a lot of money via sponsorship and live streams.

SO, WHY, TIKTOK?

In 2019, it's not really a surprise to see people who want to become famous on the internet at any cost. In fact, many people want to prove to themselves, as well as friends and family that they have what it takes to craft excellent, likeable and easily relatable contents. And this often results in being followed by many other people who admire them and the kind of content they create.

Most people put out their contents and garner followers via popular social networks such as Facebook, Instagram, Snapchat, etc. But today, a short video uploading platform called TikTok occupies an important place in people's lives.

In the past years, celebrities were all composed of actors and musicians, but today you can become famous by merely creating likeable contents and publishing them online. Some people make a career out of posting viral videos and images, and that has been proven to be a lucrative career path for those who are dedicated to it. If you ever get tired of your office work, making a career to be famous on the internet is not as crazy as it seems.

Influencers on Instagram, Snapchat and Twitter promote businesses and products on their page, and they have the liberty to charge up to six digits per publication since there is nobody to regulate the fees being charged. And then there is TikTok. The viral lip-sync app has apparently replaced the fast entertainment offered by apps such as Vine.

Becoming famous on TikTok is just like being legitimate as gaining followers only through other social media applications. But can you become famous and make money with TikTok?

Read on to discover how "celebrities" of TikTok have become famous and generated extra income. Think of Jacob Sartorius, Baby Ariel or even Loren Beech. They became famous on musical.ly by attracting the majority of users and have thus started a real career in the internet industry. Imagine if they started now on Tik Tok, which has 4 times more users than musical.ly. They would probably be followed by even more people and would have earned more and become more popular due to the large user base of this app. So this is a great opportunity for you to use this new merger between Musical.ly and TikTok to your benefit to reach a larger audience and increase your fan base.

Chapter 1
How To Get More Views And Followers On Tik Tok

So, how do you get more views in your Tik Tok videos? At first thought, you can think of "making more interesting videos", and it's a good starting point, but it's not the entire picture, it's not even close.

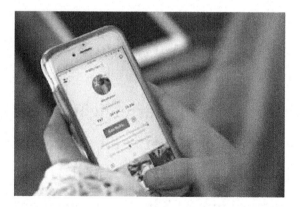

Once you familiarize yourself with the Tik Tok system, it quickly becomes crystal clear that making videos and creating contents are only part of the equation. In this book, I will show you how to increase your audience on Tik Tok in different ways.

The attracting factor for a large audience of Russian punk skate teenagers will vary from that of a large audience of Chinese rap fighters. To further enlighten you on how things work, I'll show you how to use the underlying mechanisms of Tik Tok to support your creativity and effectively promote the videos you want to make. With proper support and effective planning, your new videos will attract viewers most especially, your intended audience.

Now, let us look at how to get more views on your TikTok videos:

SET UP YOUR PROFILE

An important part of attracting an audience in their numbers is the establishment of the basics. A good profile means that a person watching one of your videos is much more likely to stay and see more, while a bad or uninformative profile will not lure a new viewer into staying and watching more of your content. The elements of a good Tik Tok profile are a sensible username, ideally, a name that expresses something about you and the type of videos that you make. "Cannabispro247" is not a good user name unless you are doing videos on cannabis, in which case makes an excellent choice for what your contents represent. Add a good picture of yourself, if you are an individual artist, or your group (if you have one). Add links to your other social networks so that people who want to connect have the choice to do so. More connections = more views. Your profile should reflect who you are and what you do with your video style, but it should also be welcoming and friendly to new viewers.

CHOOSE A NICHE

Most content creators start off on the wrong foot as they make the mistake of choosing a niche they are not so versed in due to popular demand or some other reasons. This is a wrong approach to choosing a niche, and in the end, this will create a messy brand and limit the amount of cross-attraction your videos have to prospective viewers and fans in the long run. If your fan base is dying for your polka videos then get turned off by your hip-hop content, you will never get to know if jazz rocks tickle their fancy. In addition, the 24 hours in a day is limiting for the number of videos you might want to make; this is the reason why every of your content should be up to your standard and be acceptable by your fans. If you have a unique ability, a superpower or a hidden talent, you must be ready to showcase it to the world, wow people with the things that make you unique and make money off that. There are millions of look-alike and similar sounds on Tik Tok, so you need to stand out from the crowd. So if you're an amazing drummer or you can play the piano with your toes, do it, and identify something you can do better than others and get ready to prove it over and over again.

GET SOCIAL ON SOCIAL MEDIA

Tik Tok is a social network that focuses on the social aspect of life. Watching other people's videos, watching their work, supporting them with shared interests, comments, and actions, not only boosts the person you're watching their videos but also promotes your videos. Your username appears in these comments, and if you have interesting content on your profile, people will click on your username to see what is happening in your world. You should consider being an active member of the Tik Tok community, while at it, also consider making friends and help each other to grow. Engagement is also a way to turn casual fans into hardcore fans. When you respond to someone's comment on your video positively and inclusively, it's likely to reinforce your commitment to the videos you produce.

LEVERAGE ON THE CROWN

"The crown" in Tik Tok is basically a crown icon that appears in the profiles and videos of some privileged users. Having a crown basically means that you are a recognized influencer, a mover and a shaper. There are human moderators at Tik Tok who navigate the site, looking for content creators to encourage and one of the many ways they encourage creative minds is to add a crown to such creator's profile. It will take a lot of time and effort to be successful; the crown is a reward for success, not a tool to get more. In the meantime, you should interact with the crowned characters of Tik Tok whenever you can and use their popularity to boost yours. If you leave a comment on a video that gets 100,000 views a day, your comment will be of more benefit to your TikTok career and have a much more significant impact than if you leave it on a video that gets 100 views a day.

USE TRENDING HASHTAGS

Some creators on Tik Tok can produce videos very quickly, depending on their style and niche. If you are a creator, you can use Tik Tok's trending hashtags to determine audience interest and create videos related to these hashtags.

USE CHALLENGES

Challenges are a great way to increase public participation and attract people who hear about the challenge. You can create your challenge or participate in those initiated by others. As with other social media approach, it's a good idea to do both: you want to be seen as a member of the community and as a creator in your way.

COLLABORATE

Collaboration is a big part of Tik Tok. Since the duets were introduced, it has become easier than ever to work with other people. Duets are not the only way to collaborate, but they are the simplest way to go about working with others on a project. If you find other users with a similar level of followers or someone in the same niche, offering a collaborative video project, collectively working on something amazing can win you a whole new audience. You can collaborate with people you know well or randomly interview popular creators with requests for collaboration, but do not be surprised if creators with a significantly higher audience politely (or not so politely) reject your offer; it's not personal.

POST FREQUENTLY

Social networks have incredibly short memories. Something published a day or two ago has disappeared from our consciousness unless it is exceptional or created by a celebrity. If you want to succeed in Tik Tok, you have to publish good quality videos at least once in a day. If you are actively trying to garner followers, you may need to do more. Although there is pressure to publish often, quality is always more important than quantity. It will be much better to publish less frequently but with much better quality than boring stuff all the time. Anything you do, post or say on Tik Tok will have a direct impact on the number of visitors you receive and, as a result, your number of subscribers.

LEVERAGE ON OTHER PLATFORMS

Some creators concentrate all their social media reach on Tik Tok alone, with my experience and from where I stand, I can authoritatively say that is a grave mistake. Although Tik Tok should be a great place to spend your energy, sites like Instagram and Facebook should also be significantly considered as they can turn out to be a very powerful multipliers for your audience. The reason is that, although it is possible that someone has few subscribers on Tik Tok, they could have a huge fan base on Instagram or Facebook, and if you connect with them there and also on Tik Tok, they are likely to wield the power of their fan base on these platforms to your advantage by directing people to your Tik Tok contents. Even a basic presence on other media sites can pay a lot if you keep your contents coordinated and make a lot of friends on all sites to which you participate.

Finally, be unique! Stand out from the rest of the creators. If you have nothing that can make you stand out from the crowd, you can simply copy jokes on the internet and creatively recreate them! Therefore, these are the best tips I can give you to get more views and fans on Tik Tok. This is actually a very interesting time for any user. I hope you will take advantage of this merger to leverage on the platform before every niche that will guarantee your success becomes saturated.

Chapter 2
The Way To Get Your Free
Hearts On Tiktok Now!

If you are an experienced user of Tiktok, you may want to consider your public commitment. As in all social networks, it is the commitment that makes your account live in the long run.

So you really have to consider that the behavior of your followers is very important. Getting tons of TikTok likes on your videos can help you in different ways.

BENEFITS OF LIKES ON TIKTOK

A lot of heart in your TikTok profile is instrumental when you want to attract more followers. Users will see that many people like the content you share. This is great because if they are curious enough, they may want to see your contents. Basically, this can help you reach a wider audience. Likes on TikTok is a great indicator of what your followers think of your videos. So, you can easily find out if people like to see your content or not. For example, when you find that some of the concepts in your video have many likes and comments, you will probably need to focus on them.

On the contrary, contents with a few reactions teach you what to avoid. The more likes on your TikTok profile, the more famous you will be. In fact, it's a great way to tell the difference between a big or small account. The most famous account currently has about 2 billion likes on her Tiktok profile (Loren Gray account).

Have fun with all these hearts!

HOW TO GET A VERIFIED CHECKMARK (FORMERLY CROWN) IN TIKTOK

On social platforms such as Twitter, Instagram and Facebook, some users have blue checkmarks next to their username in their profiles. Be you a celebrity, a group or an information network; these platforms place a blue checkmark next to specific pages to indicate that the accounts are verified and real. On Twitter, this is simply called "verification"; checked users are qualified as verified.

On Facebook and Instagram (owned by Facebook), there are rumors about verification. The blue ticks are called "verification badges". All three have the same goal: to show users that the account they are viewing is a real page or a parody and is not the property of fans. If you have already spent time on TikTok or Musical.ly, you have probably noticed that some users previously wore a small crown icon, next to the circular profile image that shows their face, the tiny crown disappeared from numerous profiles a few months ago.

The crowns of TikTok were relics from the time of Musical.ly, and without the crowns, you will wonder what's next? What did the crown mean? And if the crown is gone, what is replacing it? Let's take a look at where the crowns went and what they were replaced with.

WHERE WAS THE CROWN?

At the end of 2018, while everyone was celebrating Christmas and welcoming the New Year, TikTok was making a major change to its platform. A few months after the acquisition of the competing platform Musical.ly. TikTok eventually replaced the crown with a new verified verification mark, similar to other platforms.

Now that TikTok has replaced its crowns with a real verification badge, the crowns are now obsolete. In Musical.ly and earlier versions of TikTok, the crown did not only mean verified users, but also influential people and popular users of the platform. This meant that if pop stars like Selena Gomez and Ariana Grande could get their crowns, they would also find crowns awarded to users who created a brand on TikTok, video producers who demonstrate their know-how to make the service work for them and it worked well.

WHAT REPLACED CROWNS?

Instead of crowns, you will now find two different versions of the check on TikTok. The first is probably out of reach - verified user. This is the standard check that we see on most other social networks, and that is primarily reserved for celebrities to ensure that they are not supplanted. You will find this tag in some accounts, but for the most famous users of TikTok, you will find something completely new.

Instead of giving all accounts a verified badge, TikTok started to give popular Tik-Tokers a "Popular User" badge. This places these users in a higher class than the standard TikToker while stating that such a person is not a celebrity in the broadest sense of the world. TikTok does not necessarily lower the quality of the verified user; it simply means that there is now a difference between celebrities and influencers on the platform.

HOW CAN I GET VERIFIED ON TIKTOK?

As I said earlier, verification on TikTok, despite switching away from crowns, typically, these users fall into one of the three categories:

1. The user is extremely popular on the site and serves as a content creator who leaves a great mark on the TikTok platform in one way or another.

2. The user is a remarkable person, including pop stars and real musicians.

3. TikTok staff and the support team has selected them as individuals who require

verification or who have demonstrated their commitment to creating worthy content on the site.

The third option is probably your best option for getting your TikTok account verified. However, you are probably not a famous pop musician who has joined the platform. You are rather an ordinary person with a smartphone, ideas and raw talent and ready to display some level of creativity via short videos.

The good news, of course, is that you do not have to be Carly Rae Jepsen to get the popular user brand on TikTok. All you need is that raw talent and your smartphone. In fact, the path to getting verified on TikTok is quite similar to the one used to get popular on the site because the two goals are almost identical. To get a verification badge on TikTok, you will want to work to earn followers and, therefore, popularity, but that's not the end of the win. *Here are four tips to get verified quickly on TikTok:*

- **Work hard to create good content:** This is the

primary step of what you need to do to get popular and success on the site. TikTok has a large fan base, but unlike Instagram or Twitter, it's not impossible to find followers on the platform to become a big hit. TikTok is young enough so almost everyone can emerge from the shadows to become TikTok's next hit. With your videos regularly featured in the main application's feed, all you need is talent and a lot of work.

Of course, there is always a way to speed up the process, and for that, we move on to step two.

- **Follow other users to gain more followers:** As mentioned above, I have a few tips on how to win more fans/followers on TikTok, but the short version is: once you have contents that showcase your talent and creativity, you can make judicious use of the app's follow feature to get noticed by new and existing users alike. I suggest doing ten powerful TikTok clips; make it your best videos if possible and do not be afraid to try something new or out of the box. Once you are done, you can start using the title page of the app to search for new users. Refresh your feed and start searching for newly published clips of potentially successful TikTok users, possibly already crowned TikTok users. Then check out the comments on these videos to find accounts of people who like the content posted by this user. When you find a recently posted comment, click the account to add this profile to your watch list. When the user receives a notification that you have followed them, many will be inclined to visit your page and, since you already have several excellent TikTok clips on your account, that curious user is likely to follow your profile.

- **Use the right tools and the right songs:** If you are having trouble attracting targeted subscribers, make sure your TikTok videos are the best. Start by checking where you are filming. Look around and make sure you have a beautiful backdrop, outside or at home. If you are filming in your room, be sure to put things in order. Nobody wants to watch a video that takes place in a messy bedroom. Then, to improve the look of your videos, find a way to record them without having to hold your phone. It gives you the freedom of a second hand and helps you perform crazy actions without worrying about where the device is at a given time. Likewise, you must make sure that you use the right songs in your videos. You may like some songs more than others, but if you are looking for tracks that are contained only in a few videos, they will not end on the main page. If you browse TikTok's feed, you will probably notice many repetitions of songs and clips. Do not be afraid to use the same audio clips in your videos. By using popular vides, you take a step forward on the path to achieving your goal. Similarly, you can browse the search menu to find currently popular songs.

- **Don't give up:** Yes, this may seem obvious, but I've said it before: the success of any social media site starts with your efforts. There may be setbacks along the way, but if you have raw talent, you are ready to devote time and energy to content creation and work hard to promote your videos and attract a crowd, you can achieve anything with hard work and focus. Being crowned means that you have become one of the principal members of the site, a reliable person who offers incredible content with thousands of fans who follow each of your creative works. But to get there, you have to keep moving. Rome was not built in a day, as they say, and setting small goals can help you reach everything in your path. But everyone has to start somewhere, and thanks to the way TikTok rewards system, you can also begin to adapt to your goal of reaching a number of followers, likes and views. Achieving the goal of receiving a verified account on TikTok is by no means impossible.

Chapter 3
How To Get Famous On Tik Tok And Get More Likes And Views

With 1 Billion downloads on Google Play Store, TikTok is no doubt one of the most downloaded apps of 2019.

Do you want to get more followers on your TikTok profile?

Do you want to be a famous content creator on TikTok?

If your answer to these questions is yes, then you are on the right page, reading a guide that is going to change the course of your TikTok journey forever. In this chapter, I am going to discuss how you can be famous on TikTok in just 9 steps.

On a personal note, TikTok tickles my fancy, and the likes you get from fellow TikTok users is a great way to know your creativity is being appreciated. The quality of contents on TikTok will make you question if the people featured are professional actors or everyday people. Not to burst your bubble, those are people you meet on the streets day to day, the only difference is, they create their content diligently.

How To Get More Views on Your Videos:

To get more views and likes on your TikTok contents is not rocket science; however, not everyone knows how to go about it. With my experience and exposure with the platform, I can boldly say there is an 8 point agenda to achieve your set viewership goal and followership on TikTok.

1. Make judicious use of tags: **The use of trending tags to get you more views and subscribers can never be underplayed. This is also applicable to other social media platforms.**

2. Be attractive: Regardless of the niche you are in, you have to look your best every time you are making content to be uploaded on TikTok. My equation is this, the more attractive you are, the more engagement you get.

3. Take all the time you need to create your videos: there is nothing worth rushing into, creating of contents should not be rushed, and you need to take your time to ensure everything is near perfect before putting it out there for people to consume.

4. Share on other social media platforms: Your best creations should be shared on every other social media platform you are on. There is a high chance that other TikTokers will find your content outside the platform and follow you right away.

5. Pick a niche and stick with it: When you are being driven by passion, the likelihood of you to run out of ideas is slim. Choose something you love doing and back it up with hard work.

6. Casual videos and slow-mo videos mostly outperform ones made with a serious mood in mind. Nobody likes a tensed environment.

7. Get one of your female relatives or friends and make videos with her.

8. Keep on with the struggle to make it. Never give up on your goals to become famous on TikTok.

My conversation with really popular figures on TikTok about

the secrets to making it big on TikTok made me come up with a list of tips and tricks you can personally use to get famous on TikTok.

Let's take a look at them right away:

1. Look Attractive in your Videos:

Physical appearance and level of attractiveness is the first thing the human brain processes when meeting someone for the very first time. This is the same for TikTok. Research has shown that the better you look physically, the more the chances of people finding your contents pleasing to the eyes. This, in turn, leads to followers and new visitors of your profile sharing your content with their friends and colleague. The more time you spend making preparations to make your videos almost perfect, the better your chances of having that content shared by a lot of people. This will also go a long way in earning you some followers.

2. Collaborate with Famous Tik Tok Users:

This is one of the easiest ways to actually go from an underdog to being TikTok famous. A TikTok content creator with 1 million subscribers can collaborate with another with 500k followers, and that working relationship is going to benefit both sides. This is a win-win situation for both sides as they get a mutual benefit out of the collaboration. To get out of your stagnancy on TikTok, look around for people in your niche with a much larger fan base then collaborate with them, your followers are likely to increase ten times more than you had before the collaboration.

3. Add Tags To Your Video(s):

Here are some reasons why the use of tags in your TikTok videos should be greatly considered:

1. You can create your tags and make it a niche. More and more people will search for it.

2. Some tags are trending, so if you include them, then that will mean more reach of your videos.

3. People can easily find it.

4. Easy for people to find your videos in search.

5. Tags will flair your posts.

6. On the other hand, you can spinoff a content based on a tag

that is currently trending. Then, while uploading, you include the said tag in your post.

Tags play a vital role in every social media platform that is currently in existence. Let's take Twitter as a case study; the number of people who will get to see your content depends on the type of tags you use. Also, on Instagram, you use trendy tags that are related to the pictures you are posting. When you use tags that more and more people search for, you just increased the likelihood of your contents being found.

4. Tell a Funny Story:

Stories are what differentiates us from wild animals. The more stories you can tell via your content, the easier it gets for you to influence people. You cannot influence with just any story; your journey to influencing people via stories should take a comical approach. Write a script, follow it and use gestures to drive your point home within the 15secs timeframe allotted by TikTok for every video upload.

5. Using the 'For You' page:

Just like the "explore" feature on Instagram, TikTok users also have the luxury of "for you" page where users get to discover new creators and contents that might appeal to them. If you are consistent with your contents, then, you might be lucky to get featured on the "for you" page. That is the best exposure you can get for free.

6. Staying active:

No matter what you do on TikTok, if you are not active, you are not doing things the right way. When you post routinely without paying attention to how difficult it is to make contents people like, your hard work will eventually pay off. At the start of your TikTok career, creating quality content might come off as an easy job, maintaining the same quality for a very long time after you become famous might turn out to be a daunting task.

7. Using other platforms to your advantage:

To take a leaf from YouTubers, as a TikTok content creators, share your contents on other social media platforms like Facebook, Instagram, Twitter, etc. This might look strange to you, but the benefits are unlimited. For starters, your content will get more exposure, and your target audience will eventually go to your TikTok channel and hopefully subscribe to your work. While uploading on other platforms, do not forget to include your TikTok profile link as, without that, your efforts are more or less a waste.

· Linking your other social media accounts to your TikTok profile will help people to find you easily.

· You can opt to advertise your content on other social media platforms.

I hope this chapter has imparted some knowledge you find useful into your journey to becoming famous on TikTok?

Chapter 4
How To Earn Money From Tiktok

How to Earn Money From
TikTok

Being famous on TikTok comes at a price, and here is a rough estimate of how much you can make as a famous TikToker.

If you had no idea you could make money on TikTok before now, congratulations to you for finding this book. All you have to do is read to the end to benefit from the knowledge I am about to share.

Before we proceed, you need to know the basics of TikTok and how to get your contents on it.

How to Make Good Videos on TikTok

Similar to every other social media platform, you have to create a user account on the TikTok platform. To do that, you can download the app on Google Play Store or Apple Store.

To create a TikTok profile, launch the app you just downloaded, select the "me" option. You will be presented with the option to sign up with either your Gmail, Facebook, Twitter or Instagram account. Alternatively, your phone number can be used to sign up.

How to Earn Money from TikTok (Musical.ly)?

Back to what got us here – how to make money from TikTok.

To create a 15 – 30seconds video on TikTok, you only have to shoot for an hour or thereabout. If you can make money with such a not-so-demanding task, then, it is a great avenue for you to make some extra income.

Without further ado, let's jump right into how you can make money from TikTok platform.

Unlike Youtube, TikTok does not have a monetization feature, the question that is probably on your mind now is, how then can one earn? To answer your question, I have highlighted some ways you can make money on TikTok;

1. Live Streaming

This is the most basic way to earn money on TikTok. How does this work? There is an inbuilt TikTok feature that allows you to live stream your content to your fans.

On the other hand, there is a paid emoji feature – this allows your fans to buy emojis at a fixed rate. These emojis can then be sent to you during your live streams. When you get emojis, it will be converted into coins on your account, and you can convert them to real money that will be deposited into your bank account. Before the live stream feature can be activated on the profile of any TikTok content creator, they must have 1,000 followers.

2. Hashtag Contest

There are numerous contests in the TikTok app you can take part in. One of these contests is the "hashtag contest" and if you happen to win this contest, your content will get featured in the trending videos section, and you will stand a chance to win prizes like $100, $1000 coupons, TikTok tools or mobile phones.

3. Gifts

If you have a lot of followers and you drive huge traffic to the platform, the company will send you gifts. These gifts have great values, and you can decide to sell them to get their worth in cash.

4. Sponsorship

Similar to Youtube, you can earn money from sponsorships. Brands and companies can choose to sponsor your contents, and you earn money via that.

5. Becoming an influenza

Just like Instagram, with your large fan base, you can promote other people's brand or product and make some cash out of it.s

This is the end of the tips on how to make money on TikTok. Hope you have learnt a thing or two from the information contained in this chapter. If you like what you have read above, be kind enough to share with every TikToker you know so that they too can also make money off the platform. Remember, sharing is caring.

CONCLUSION

At the end of it all, the most crucial step to being successful on TikTok is to give it your all and never give up. The merge of Musical.ly and TikTok has made the platform more popular as a large number of new users sign up every day on the platform. Be active and keep your contents fresh and lively.

To end it all, you must come to the realization that nothing in this life is hard; all you have to do is to condition your mindset to never give up. I am certain these tips that I have churned out will help you to grow your TikTok account in no time and also help you become famous on TikTok as soon as possible.

Talk again soon,

Nina

OTHER BOOKS BY THE AUTHOR:

HOW TO CANCEL AMAZON PRIME
SUBSCRIPTION: A Step by step
Solution on how to Cancel Amazon
Prime Subscription with Screenshots

https://www.amazon.com/dp/B07KVL2
823

HOW TO RETURN A KINDLE
UNLIMITED BOOK IN 3 STEPS: A 3-
Step Solution on how to Return
Borrowed Kindle book With
Screenshots

https://www.amazon.com/dp/B07
9W3H65G

KINDLE UNLIMITED: Is It Worth The
Price?: READ TO FIND OUT!!

https://www.amazon.com/dp/B07
9DFZT4Y

Thanks

For

Reading....

Made in the USA
Monee, IL
18 December 2019

19002684R00046